Directions *to* Destiny

STACEY SPELLER
Author of *The Designer Life*

Directions *to* Destiny

A ROADMAP TO FINDING TRUE LOVE

Copyright © 2018 by Stacey Speller
All rights reserved. This book or any portion thereof may not be reproduced or used in any manner whatsoever without the express written permission of the publisher except for the use of brief quotations in a book review.

Printed in the United States of America

Second Edition, 2018

ISBN 978-0-9798916-6-3 (Print Version)
ISBN 978-0-9798916-7-0 (Electronic Version)

Speak2Stacey, LLC
10 GlenLake Parkway, Suite 130
Atlanta, GA. 30328
www.staceyspeller.com

Editing and Proofreading by Nhat Crawford
(nhatcrawford@gmail.com)

Book Cover, Layout and Typesetting by Vanessa Mendozzi

Contents

CHAPTER 1 - THE DIRECTIONAL ROADMAP	1
CHAPTER 2 - WHO ARE YOU?	15
CHAPTER 3 - WHY ARE YOU?	25
CHAPTER 4 - WORK FROM THE INSIDE OUT	45
CHAPTER 5 - OKAY BY YOURSELF- UNPLUG THE LIFE SUPPORT	55
CHAPTER 6 - WHAT'S IN YOUR TRUNK?	69
CHAPTER 7 - ARE YOUR READY FOR THE JOURNEY?	77
CHAPTER 8 - IS YOUR VEHICLE WELL MAINTAINED FOR THE TRIP?	85
CHAPTER 9 - WHAT TO KNOW BEFORE YOU GO	95
CHAPTER 10 - STRIKE GOLD ALONG THE WAY	101
CHAPTER 11 - WHY ARE YOU GOING THERE?	107
CHAPTER 12 - DOES THAT CAR LOOK LIKE IT WILL MAKE THE TRIP?	113
CHAPTER 13 - CLASSICS ARE STILL GOOD FOR THE TRIP	117
CHAPTER 14 - BE CAREFUL OF THE BLIND SPOTS	125
CHAPTER 15 - WHERE IS TRUE LOVE ANYWAY?	137

To Kyle

Because of you I know that love is not a theory but a series of never ending selfless acts. Continue to follow your dreams for I am amazed and inspired by your relentless pursuit to accomplish your goals. I love you around the world and back again.

Mom

CHAPTER 1

The Directional Roadmap

Welcome to what I hope will be your roadside assistance for your life journey. Realizing that as women we have so many complexities that we factor into our various relationships, I wanted to make a difference for others based on life experience and wisdom from God. I am now keenly aware that I have been blessed beyond measure in matters of the heart and it is my firm belief that we are blessed to bless others, so I pray that my blessing will soon become yours as well.

Many of the topics covered in this book were instilled in me as a child and for that I am eternally grateful, not only to my parents, but also to my village. Knowing the importance of loving God, learning how to love myself, knowing who I am, believing in my abilities, and appreciating inner beauty are all a part of the foundation that was poured for my life since the beginning of my assignment here on earth. For as long as I can remember, I was taught the basic principles that are discussed at length in this book. Fortunately, I was an excellent student and learned my lessons well.

My father was an undercover homicide detective known for quoting everything from the Bible to ancient proverbs. His very straight-forward, matter of fact personality became a part of the frame of reference I needed when times were tough. I can remember my first day of intense teasing in first grade and coming home in tears with a resolution that I would never return to school. Dad's loving response to me regarding the negative talk from my classmates was, "They talked bad about a perfect Jesus and said nothing good would come out of Nazareth. What on earth makes you think they won't talk about you?"

During another social lull in my young life I looked around to find that I was alone, without any playmates, and naturally I complained about it. Dad's response was, *"You came into this world with you and God, and you will leave this world with you and God; it is best if you learn how to be okay with you and God while you are here."* However, the ultimate piece of advice came when I thought my heart was broken beyond repair, and I was left with a life doomed to misery by my eighth grade crush David. As I recited the details of a crush gone badly to my father, he promptly distilled it with, *"Anything in life that doesn't kill you will make you stronger."*

My mother also did not hesitate to dispense nuggets of wisdom. For instance, when I began dating she wold always remind me that, *everything that is good to you isn't good for you*. I am grateful for what I know is truth because wisdom and experience have become my friends and I embrace them wholeheartedly. Imagine that you can live long enough to appreciate some of the things your parents tried to teach you.

Many of my friends have often asked me how I have avoided so many pitfalls in life. There are only two explanations I can ever offer. The most prevalent one is prayers that come from a righteous person. You might have read it yourself; *the effectual, fervent prayers of a righteous person avail much* and I know for a fact that a lot of righteous people prayed for me! Secondly, the African proverb that says, *It takes a village to raise a child*, was applied during my upbringing quite liberally as I was blessed with an intensely wise village that imparted wisdom-filled lessons to me from lengthy lifetimes of experience from these loving villagers.

Nonetheless, I did not escape personal challenges. They came like a tumultuous wind whipping me about just like anyone else. One of the more valuable lessons I remember is that in life it is not what happens to you, it is what you do with it. Like most women, I have had my "he did me wrong" experience too, but I chose to learn from it and to become all the better for it.

In my early twenties, I dated a guy named Rob who seemed to be a nice Christian gentleman. Rob was about 8 years older than I was which at the time seemed like a big age difference but I went out with him because he was very kind, extremely polite and always suggested nice date places. When I had met Rob, I believed him to be single with no children and I began to really like him. Well, one evening while having dinner with him, a very pregnant woman approached our table with tears streaming down her face and confronted Rob. As ill chance would have it, this woman was engaged to Rob, was the mother of his three year old son and was seven months pregnant with their second child!

During the confrontation Rob convinced this woman to sit down at the table with us to avoid making a scene although in hindsight it seems to me that a scene should have been the least of his worries. Rob begins to explain that he and I are simply business acquaintances and it is not what she thought. This brought me to a real moment of truth; there was a part of me that wanted to play into Rob's story in order to spare his fiancé's feelings. Yet another part of me considered that she was about to marry a liar and a cheat, which could not have possibly been a good thing for her in the long run.

In that instant I opted to tell her the truth about Rob and me; that we had actually been dating for several months (because I thought he was single with no children) What unraveled next left me speechless, but more importantly, it left the kind of imprint on my life that will potentially help others. The woman immediately turned all of her anger on me and began to call me clearly what my parents had not named me. Then with a nervy resolve, she completely absolved Rob of any fault or blame. Fortunately I had the presence of mind to get up and leave the restaurant—equally as fortunate, because of my mother's teachings, I had my own money with me and was able to catch a cab home.

As the dust began to settle around what had happened, of course I experienced all of the natural emotions one would expect. I was humiliated, angry, embarrassed, and hurt. But, more importantly, it left me curious as to why the woman had turned on me as if I were the perpetrator of wrongdoing in her relationship with Rob. I began to wonder, wasn't he the one that had fathered her children and yet denied their existence to me? Rob was the one that had asked for her hand in marriage, and I am sure, had promised her faithfulness and honesty among other things. The man she obviously knew intimately and was in love with had violated her trust and cheated on her yet she was angry at me—a perfect stranger!

Over time I came to understand more of the dynamics that were at work here both with Rob and his fiancé. Many of the issues are discussed directly and indirectly in this book. Many years later I ran into Rob and due to the environment where I saw him, (church) I was able to muster enough Christian decency to respond to his hello. Of course he informed me that he and his fiancé had indeed married and now had three children.

Rob was even concerned enough about his own need to feel forgiven that he wanted me to acknowledge that I didn't have any hurt feelings. I promptly assured him that he, nor the incident, meant anything to me at all. After all someone like Rob does not even deserve the self-satisfaction of believing either he or his actions made an lasting impression on me.

The great blessing during that time was the godly counsel that flowed from the members of my village toward me. They proved to be sufficient help as I quickly recovered from the Rob fiasco. But what I have learned is that many women are not so fortunate; they have debilitating problems that impeded the movement necessary for their journey. Now mind you, some of the troubles are self-inflicted, and some are a result of not having good directions before setting out on the trip. Either way, I knew that it was important to acknowledge that at different times we all need a little navigational assistance, which certainly makes it okay to stop and get directions to our destiny.

While deciding on a title for this book, I prayed about what would be a marketable, catchy title that would not water down the expression of my faith. I tested the title with family and close friends and received favorable responses from them. Most people were not quite sure what I was writing the book about, but, knowing me as they do, they assumed the general theme would be about faith, women, relationships, or all of the above. Indeed that is the general theme here. More specifically, the reason for this writing springs from a very heartfelt need that I discovered through life coaching, as well as, through my own personal experiences.

I came to realize how deeply women were hurting and that they didn't quite understand how they ended up on the wrong road headed to nowhere. I knew there had to be a way to reach the feminine masses with a message of assurance that we can all get lost from time to time and need directions to find our destination. We typically think of men who won't stop and ask for street directions, but, in the way of love and relationships, women too often fail to seek direction as well. Even worse, we often ask people who are as lost as we are. Taking the time to make sure you have accurate directions will save you precious time and energy along the journey we call life.

After high school graduation, I moved to southern California to attend college and did not have a clue about how to read a map. Having lived in

Philadelphia my entire life, reading a map had not become an acquired skill because it was totally unnecessary. In Philadelphia everything is geographically close together with not more than a scant 15-minute-drive to anywhere you need to go. Most of the time you already know how to get where you want to be, and if not, asking directions is a given; simple" turn left" or "turn right" instructions get you to your destination.

Not so in my new home on the other side of the country, away from what I'd always known. Moving to southern California opened me up to a whole new world in traveling from point A to point B. I discovered 20 different freeways with names and numbers that traveled every direction on the compass. Some even traveled in a combination of different directions. Every direction, road, street, and neighborhood was widely spread out from one another, and when natives indicated something wasn't geographically far, that typically meant there was just a little less than one hour of driving time involved.

When I arrived in California, I soon became perpetually lost and had to constantly ask for directions. When giving me directions, some people referred to the freeway by name and others by number. As if that wasn't challenging enough, I had to figure out which freeway to travel, depending upon the name or the number. Additionally, Californians use compasses to find their way and give out directions to others accordingly; they tell you to get off the freeway and go north. Or, worse still, they tell you to go towards the mountains or the ocean! Now I ask you, how does a turn-left or turn-right Philly girl know what to do when the only direction she has are to get off the freeway and go north? After all, there are clearly no mountains or ocean in Philadelphia. So, there I was riding around unable to understand the path I was on, lost and going nowhere fast.

And last, one of the most liberating things happened when I admitted that I didn't know where I was going, which had fueled my being lost all the time.

My dad taught me how to read a map. What a novel concept. I was so excited I bought two maps-one for the house and one to keep in the car. In California, the map book is the same size as a phonebook in most metropolitan cities, so learning to read it was no easy task, but well worth it. Armed with my map in the car, if I got lost, I could stop and get directions to my destination. I now see life in the same way as using the California map book. It is far better to invest the time in learning how to read the map book and get directions than to wander around through love and life lost, not knowing your way.

It is my sincere desire for this book to assist you in discovering your own unique directions toward peace, love, and joy. And just as I often wondered who is in charge of the map book company that provided the data of so many freeways and streets, you too may wonder who is in charge of all my data; quite simply, God is the author and finisher of my data.

CHAPTER 2

Who Are You?

Who are you? As you set out on the journey of life and begin going from here to there you have to know your starting point where you are. One of the most important things you can spend time doing for yourself is getting to know and understand who you are, Whose you are and why you are. The time you spend getting to know yourself will uncover what your true likes and dislikes are. What are your specific needs? What are your values and priorities? What makes you happy? While this may seem simplistic on the surface, the fact is so many women are not able to articulate who they are and what they want out of life. Many women that I coach are not even able to readily describe what makes them happy as an individual, outside of friends and family. This is a very interesting dynamic because truthfully speaking, how will you ever be able to properly discern if a potential mate is suitable for you if you don't even know who you are?

Kim is a 42 year old single woman, with a Master's Degree in Accounting, a thriving accounting practice, and homeowner, with no children and has never been married before. When Kim hired me as her coach, primarily her focus was on getting the help she needed to identify and ultimately conquer what ever it was that she felt was sabotaging her personal dating life.

When I asked Kim what makes her happy, she indicated that pleasing her parents, being around her family and hanging out with her friends made her happy. There is nothing wrong with any of this, but then I asked Kim specifically what makes her happy in and of herself without factoring anyone else into the formula. Kim was unable to tell me anything that made her happy or any activity or hobby that did not require the involvement of her family and/or friends.

Through several months of coaching, Kim and I worked diligently to discover what made her happy and eventually we moved on to determine her wants and needs as well as her core values that she wasn't willing to compromise on. Now imagine if Kim had met and began to date during the time she was trying to get to know herself. She would not have been able to bring her authentic self into a relationship because she didn't even know who her authentic self was.

More importantly, if you are not able to articulate your wants and needs, how will anyone you are involved in a relationship with be able to meet your needs? Most men can (and do) become frustrated by the mystery and complexities of women. What makes it even more difficult is when they believe they are trying their best to do things that are pleasing to us and it seems as though they are failing. Often, the men are failing because we don't even know what would be pleasing to us.

I have come to realize that chronological age and maturity help with the endeavor of discovering who you really are. While it is imperative to know who you are at any age, the more we mature as women, the more likely we are to stop trying to be who we think other people want us to be and become more comfortable in who we truly are. As you discover who you are, you can learn how to become comfortable in your own skin. This is liberation in the true sense of the word. When you are able to know yourself and be comfortable with who you are, then you are well on the way to becoming open to invite others into your life.

One of my clients, Tina, would always yield to her husband when it came time to select something as simple as a restaurant for dinner or a movie. When her husband would ask Tina where she wanted to dine she would always indicate that it didn't matter and wherever he wanted to go was fine with her. If Tina and her husband were going to the movies, she would always yield to what her husband indicated he wanted to see at the movies. Now Tina's husband loved action films and yet Tina could not openly and honestly admit that she didn't like action films at all.

Tina's husband began to feel like he was not ever doing anything nice for Tina because she would never articulate her wants when it came to their date nights. When Tina questioned me regarding this, I asked her what it would be like for her to pick the restaurant or the movie. She had never even considered making suggestions or asserting her requests because she had not ever spent the time deciding what she really liked. This is a case of someone who did not know who she was prior to entering into a relationship.

Eventually, Tina became comfortable selecting

restaurants and making movie suggestions that suited her as well. Turns out she enjoyed comedies and love stories. Tina's husband had wanted to please her, but was hindered by Tina's lack of self knowledge independent of anyone or anything else.

As you begin getting to really know yourself, spend some time asking yourself these questions:

- How grounded am I in my relationship with God?
- How do I live out my faith?
- What things are important to me?
- What things are insignificant to me?
- What types of food do I enjoy?
- What movies do I enjoy?
- What are my hobbies?
- How important is it to me that I have the approval of others?
- Do I enjoy traveling and if so where do I like to go?
- Do I enjoy sports and if so which ones?

- » Do I like to read and if so what types of books do I enjoy?
- » How do I like to spend my quiet time?
- » Do I enjoy being around large groups or small intimate gatherings?
- » Am I a morning person or a night owl?
- » What's important in my living environment?
- » Am I entrepreneur minded?
- » If I did not work in my current line of work, what else would I do?
- » If money were not a consideration, how would I like to spend my time?
- » What am I the most proud of having accomplished?

Of course the list could go on forever but the purpose is to really ask yourself the type of questions that really help you discover yourself. Consider this an open invitation to spend time getting to know the innermost you and don't be surprised by what you might discover. Many of us are not even living up to a fraction of the potential God has given us.

Just remember that when you know better who you are, you must then do better with what you have.

When I was in college, a guy I was dating asked me to go the Lakers basketball game. Now, I was never a sports fan at all and had absolutely no interest in watching any sports, whether live or on television. Even now I sometimes amaze myself that I am able to support my teenage son by attending his games and tournaments like the most diligent of fans. When this guy asked me to attend the Lakers game, because I had not yet taken time to know myself well, I agreed to the date.

After all I had a plan to entertain myself for what I assumed would only be a few hours. Since I love to read and can always entertain myself with a good novel, I took my book with me to the game and thought it was perfectly acceptable for me to sit and read while he watched the basketball game. Right there in my court-side seat I pulled out a book and began to read. Within minutes my date's face changed completely. His shock and disbelief over my choice to read at his beloved Lakers game was quite obvious as he asked me what I was doing. My response to him carried just as much shock that he didn't understand that I was reading so that he could watch the game.

Needless to say the evening did not go well since he wanted me to show interest in the game and I preferred to ready my book. The date ended quite early with not much hope by either of us for a second meeting.

After consulting several sports fans, I was informed of how outrageous it was for me to read a book while sitting court-side at a Lakers Game. I am now able to understand that perhaps if I had spent some time getting to know myself, what was important to me, as well as what I enjoyed and didn't enjoy, this whole situation could have been avoided.

At that point in my life, I was operating on cruise

control and going through the motions of life without any real thought or regard for my real "who." Looking back on the situation I can clearly see that I should have declined the invitation to the game and encouraged him to take someone who enjoyed basketball and then I could have suggested a different date alternative for the two of us. Instead this is just a very simple yet classic example of what can happen in life and relationships. If you are not sure about who you are and what you want, you just might end up somewhere you don't want to be.

CHAPTER 3

Why Are You?

Consider this. A fruitful garden calls for good soil; once a seed has been planted, it must be nurtured and cared for. Similarly, a seed has been planted in each of us so you may want to ask yourself, how fertile or good is my soil because surely this is what it takes for a seed to take root and grow. How are you caring for the seed God has planted inside of you? I trust you have given thought to who you are, and now you will want to discover *why* you are. The *why* you are speaks to your general purpose in life.

Purpose in the context of this book refers to the

reason *you believe* you exist. I have met many single women who sincerely believe that their one true purpose in life is to find a mate. While I cannot tell you what your purpose is, I can assure you that your purpose is not finding a mate. Perhaps finding a mate is a goal, but it is not, nor will it ever be, the purpose for your existence. Consider that God formed you in His perfect image as a complete and whole being of spirit, soul and body.

To believe that your value is limited to finding someone else to fulfill and complete your life is a falsehood perpetuated by our popular culture. Certainly there isn't anything wrong with meeting that special someone to share your life with, but you must begin with your whole complete self walking in your own unique purpose.

Since purpose was defined as that thing for which *you believe* you exist, the operative words are you believe. Be careful not to confuse purpose with vision. Purpose is a belief that you have. If you're not careful, it can be manufactured based on personal desire. A strong personal desire for something can sometimes cloud our purpose. Vision, however, is given by God and cannot be man-made or manufactured. Once God gives you a vision, you will then come into alignment and understanding regarding your purpose.

The Bible tells us that where there is no vision, the people shall perish. Clearly if perishing is the outcome for lack of vision, it should not be taken lightly, especially since the Bible also tells us to write the vision and make it plain. I cannot stress enough how crucial it is to spend time with God to get your vision. You cannot expect a man of vision, purpose, and destiny to want a relationship with someone who can't even see her way out of a paper bag.

When you know who you are, there must be a vision along with an accompanying roadmap that leads to your personal destination. In order to get where God wants to take you, there must be a vision and a plan for your life that will develop into purpose and destiny. Therefore, purpose should be the living, breathing manifestation of the vision that God has given you with plans and goals simply to guide the way.

The destiny of your purpose should include dreams that constantly grow and evolve as your life does. I always love when guest of the Oprah Winfrey show indicate that they had always dreamed of meeting her because she turns around and encourages them to go and dream an even bigger dream!

Vision may not make sense to you right here and now. You may think to yourself, *"I would have never thought of something like this!"* or *"This just doesn't fit my life"* or even, *"I don't know how I would ever accomplish that."* If your vision makes perfect sense and allows you to see exactly how it is going to come to pass, chances are it is not the vision God has for you. Instead it is an over-active imagination.

If His thoughts are not our thoughts and His ways are higher than our ways, we cannot possibly believe that we would immediately be able to grasp everything He has for us all at one time. In fact, I believe that if we knew the entire plan before the journey, chances are we would never take the trip. Sometimes we are so busy and our lives are filled with so much static that we are not able to grasp the vision because we don't have time to pay attention to it. At times like these, don't be surprised if God has to slow you down in order for you to catch the vision. The storms of life force us to earnestly seek God in prayer, and that is when God knows we are most attentive to His gentle whisper.

One of my coaching clients, Paula, had a very powerful career in corporate banking. She was married with one grown child and had sacrificed her personal enjoyment in life for her corner office with a view of the city. Paula planned out every detail of her life according to what she thought she wanted to accomplish-the American dream. She had even planned to have only one child because she did not want limitations on her career.

Aside from that, she could not embrace the thought of having a houseful of children. One day Paula's perfectly planned world began to unravel around her. She was downsized out of her job and one of her elderly parents became very ill. It was during this time that God had Paula's attention, and she began to pray for His will and vision for her life. Paula and I began working together as she developed clarity around what she would do next. She wanted a Christian coach because she felt a strong leading towards something different, yet she felt uncertain about it.

Paula began to share with me that she had a vision that she was supposed to teach. The problem for Paula was that it didn't make sense. The vision was completely out of sync with her thirty-plus years of banking, her education in finance, and her perceived skills. When we were finally able to work through the concept that vision doesn't have to make sense to us as long as it comes from God, Paula became free to take action.

She went back to school and earned her master of education degree and began teaching. Once Paula was in the classroom she realized that her real gift was with students who have special needs. Paula then took a job with an alternative high school where her students were at risk for dropping out of school. She teaches them vocational education and life skills to help them see the value of completing their high school education.

Recently, Paula was awarded federal grant money to begin her own charter school for troubled children. While Paula's season for banking and finance was all part of shaping who she is, now that she is operating in God's vision, she tells me that she has never been happier. She now has more time for both her husband and her parents, with time off during the summer to spend with her new granddaughter. Paula is living out her purpose based on the vision God already had for her life. If Paula had rationalized away her vision, the purpose would have never manifested.

Instead, Paula trusted the vision God gave her and did not rely on her own very limited viewpoint of what seemed to make sense at the time. On your journey, always take comfort in the fact that God's sight is better than your sight, so let Him take command of the vehicle.

When I began writing this book, I knew that I could not even begin professing to have all the answers regarding purpose. Nor do I believe that this book is the panacea or the silver bullet to discovering your "why" in life. There are any number of books available that are geared toward finding out your purpose with step-by-step instructions and workbooks to guide you through the process. Because knowing your purpose is just one component of the roadmap, suffice it to say this book is not the final authority on purpose.

What I can offer, however, is a very honest and transparent glimpse into what I know as my truth and my journey to discover my God-given purpose and passion. I pray that by sharing my experience, I will help inspire others to seek out the directions for their own destiny.

I discovered my purpose once I began to realize that I was blessed with gifts and talents for a reason and that it was my duty to find out the best use of my existence. It is so easy when you are single to believe that your purpose will come with marriage and children. When you are married, it is very easy to believe that you are living your purpose by being married with children.

What I discovered is that purpose is not a team sport. This is not to suggest that you will not work with others to accomplish the manifestation of your purpose, but it does mean that true purpose is individual and personal between you and God. One of my favorite books of the Bible is the book of Esther, and as I began to walk in my purpose I always thought of Queen Esther….. *Coming to the kingdom for such a time as this.* Your purpose and your *why* should require the sense of *such a time as this*; regardless of what else has happened and will happen, "this is what I should be doing."

As you are living inside of your *why*, notice that your purpose gives you energy. Not that you won't ever feel tired, but true purpose is energizing; you are glad to do it because you know it is why you are who you are. I believe that your purpose is always there as a part of your spiritual DNA; it is just a matter of *Why* meeting *When*. And so when I began coaching and speaking, I knew it was the culmination of my gifts, talents, and experiences meting with timing and opportunity.

I cannot remember a time when I was not interacting with people, helping them to analyze their situations and to solve their problems. Most of my friends from elementary school, through college, and beyond always remember me encouraging and motivating them through whatever was needed at the time. In the early 1970's, long before call-waiting, cell phones, the internet or any other modern communication amenities, I had my own phone line in my room.

When I was ten years old, my father could no longer tolerate that, whenever he either called home or needed to use the phone, the line was always busy. Thus he did what was unheard of for that time and had my own phone line installed in my room. I believe something as simple as a phone line was the launching pad for discovering my purpose. Now I could talk on the phone for hours on end. Without any interruption I could motivate and encourage my friends.

In fact, the impetus for the naming of my company comes from that phone experience. When my dad presented me with the phone, he instructed me to have all of my friends call my new number so he could live in peace without having to constantly hear, "May I speak to Stacey?" While my college experience/education and previous career path were not geared towards coaching, speaking, or writing, they were preparation for my purpose. I needed the valuable life experience to be even more effective in what I do now. Through my faith I was able to truly see my why; that the gifts and talents I possess are for what God had purposed for me. It was time for my *why* to meet my *when*. Perhaps you are ready to introduce your *why* to your *when*.

Your chosen career path may or may not be your purpose. Chances are, if you do not get any enjoyment or fulfillment from your chosen career, or your business, it is very likely that you are not living out your purpose. You should never feel miserable in your why and on some level there should be a sense of gratification and satisfaction. Perhaps you have not discovered your *why* because you thought there might somehow be a perceived, very complex and profound process for your *why*. This was true in my case because I over dramatized the entire concept.

While, yes, for some people there are purposes that are a very specific call on our life where the message is very precise for example, knowing that you must discover the cure for cancer or the cause of Alzheimer's disease are great, distinct, and specific purposes that I believe someone is truly called to do. Others are clearly instructed, by God through the Holy Spirit, of an exact roadmap for what He wants us to do and how we are to go about it. Then there are those of us who have to take away all of the mystery of our *why* and trust God that it just is.

I spent several years struggling to find my purpose because I was expecting a great parting of the heavens, the sound of a loud trumpet, and God Himself peeking through the clouds to tell me, *"Stacey! This is what I want you to do!"* I have read accounts of people having experiences similar to this; however, for me it was more of an intuitive, gentle whisper that provided the direction I needed to start moving along the path that was set for me.

The movement on the correct path is critical because sometimes we are set on the path but then we don't move. We become immobile for fear of failure, success, or worse; fear of what others might think of our journey. When I didn't immediately move on my path, I constantly thought of the quote from Will Rogers, "Even if you're on the right track, you'll get run over if you just sit there." Certainly, movement and action are required on our part to fully manifest our purpose.

When you have discovered why you exist and what you must accomplish, you have to identify what you are willing to do in order to authentically live out the ultimate potential of your purpose. I say *authentically* because for so many of us, life can be one enormous masquerade party where we walk around with a false persona to mask who we really are. Consider for a moment how much energy you need and how big a bridge you must build to cover the gap between who you really are and who you want everyone to think you are.

Now imagine for a moment what you would accomplish if you channeled your bridge-building energy into your God-given purpose. Certainly on some level we have all either attended the masquerade party or we know someone who has. I was once a regular attendee at the party. For so many of us, our costumes for the masquerade party were selected during our formative years. Perhaps our parents or other family members had such a profound influence on us, both good and bad, that we became what we thought was expected of us. Something from our past experience helped shape which character we would take on and wear to the masquerade party.

During my teenage years, my grandmother instilled in me a great sense of household neatness and order due to her conviction that it made you better at everything else in your life. She clearly believed that how neat and clean you kept your home was a direct reflection on your overall worth as a person. If cleanliness were truly next to godliness, then grandmother was godly in a way that most of us can only dream of. As a teenager, I used to watch her clean the inside burners of a gas stove with a Q-tip and ammonia. She washed clothes daily and ironed everything, including sheets and workout clothes. By the time I was in my early twenties, I had proudly adopted my grandmother's way of housekeeping, and I became very proud of my perfect, obsessively clean, and anal house. When life began to happen and I became exceptionally busy, my husband decided we should hire a cleaning service to help free up some of our time. Of course I didn't want the cleaning people to believe that I couldn't maintain my house in a neat and orderly way, so I began to build my bridge.

The day before the cleaning service came I would go into over drive making sure everything was put away neatly, the closets were organized, all of the dishes were put away, and every thing was arranged perfectly in the cabinets. I even fussed at my husband and son if they left something sitting out of place before the cleaning service arrived. Never mind that I was in school full-time, helping my husband run his business that was fifty miles from our home, maintaining the household bills and errands, and commuting my son to school and practices.

In one year I put over 55,000 miles on my car without any planned road trips or vacations. In fact, my car had not left the state where we live. My costume for the masquerade party required me to do it all and have it all, and that is what I needed to project to the world. Although the analogy of the cleaning people may seem lightweight, the theme of trying so hard to be who we want people to believe we are is a serious concept. I could have used all of that cleaning energy and badgering of my family for something far more productive towards my purpose.

That is why truth in purpose is so important. The truth of the matter is that I was too busy with my career change, my husband's business and our son, that I didn't have time to be a good housekeeper.

How liberating and profound to actually let the cleaning people come to my house and do what they were getting paid to do-clean. Walking in our purpose requires us to stop pretending and live with our true self. Don't be afraid to change direction if you realize that the purpose you thought was for you actually belonged to someone else. It is okay to come into that revelation as long as you are willing to do something as radical as make a change. Accept that it is okay to have a chink in the armor and that purpose doesn't require perfection. Remember, purpose is what you are doing as you manifest the vision. Because you are involved, it will not always be perfect. The perfection comes in your vision from God.

During one of my coaching courses in school, one of the first models we learned was the Who, What, How model. The theory behind this model is that when you focus on the who and the what, the how will manifest. I know that as you get to know who you truly are and what God has purposed for you, your *how* will begin to surface in ways that you could not even imagine. My personal testimony is a living, breathing example of the Who, What, How model. When I began to understand and then acknowledge who I really was and what God had given me as the vision for my life, the strategy of how my vision would get accomplished became abundantly clear and my job was to begin walking in it.

I began coaching clients almost immediately after completing my training; I was invited to speaking engagements that generated more coaching clients; I was asked to write a column in my local newspaper and eventually a magazine and now I have written my first book with other books on the way. God has blessed me tremendously and manifested the vision without my having to spend time agonizing over how it was going to happen. When you are faithful to God, He is faithful to you. As you are on your journey of vision and purpose, always remember, it is okay to stop and get directions along the way to your destiny.

CHAPTER 4

Work From The Inside Out

Now that you are comfortable in your who, what, why and where, you can begin loving and valuing yourself from the inside out. As you consider traveling on the road to love, you want to begin equipping yourself for the journey, carrying the confidence and self-assurance needed for sharing the wonderful you with the rest of the world. This process begins with the inner you. Begin to examine how proficient you are at being secure within yourself. This is a critical skill to master because without a well-built, secure foundation, the house is sure to fall apart. I believe that confidence and self assurance are abilities that we learn over time and constantly need to refine along the way.

As life happens, it is probable that all of us will have periods of self-doubt. While occasional questioning of oneself is normal, letting it affect us negatively, and taking on a less-than-worthy attitude are detrimental. How certain we feel about ourselves should not fluctuate according to the problems that are bound to surface; therefore, we want to learn how to walk in a continuous state of confidence. I strongly encourage my coaching clients to keep a journal for documenting triumphs and blessings to reflect upon when the storms of life are raging and circumstances make it challenging to remember your confidence.

Unfortunately, I meet many women who have a very difficult time affirming themselves and are in a seemingly endless state of low self-confidence. This is extremely unfortunate because lack of confidence on the inside is very visible on the outside. Consider how much a lack of confidence can negatively impact your witness. Imagine if you didn't know Jesus as your Savior and you interacted with your co-worker who always talked about loving Jesus and going to church, yet she was lacking self-esteem and confidence all the time. Would you want to consider a life with Christ? Probably not. So, if for no other reason than your personal witness, you want to improve in the area of feeling good about you in order to be a good representative of the kingdom of God.

One evening I was watching a television news program on teenagers and the problems they face in America today. The show's host indicated that gangs, depression, suicide, and promiscuity were just some of the crises that young people are now faced with. Most of the teens who were interviewed on the show admitted to having low self-esteem and no confidence in themselves. At the end of the show, the commentator stressed how important it was for concerned parents to speak with their teenagers about these issues.

As a concerned parent of a teenager, I spoke with my son Kyle regarding what I had seen. I began asking him about peer pressure, bullies, and other students at school who might have made him feel bad about himself. Kyle seemed very surprised that I was asking him this and asked me how someone else would go about doing that to him. So I explained what I had just seen on the news program and that perhaps through teasing or some other method, there were people at school who possibly made him feel bad.

I have always known that Kyle is very precocious and has all of the characteristics of an only child who has spent too much time with adults, but his answer surprised even me. Kyle very politely told me that the reason it is called self-esteem is that the emphasis is on the fact that it comes from self; that however you feel, good or bad, it is because of what you have allowed yourself to feel. He then went on to tell me that if he let other people contribute to what he thought of himself, then it would be called group-esteem, not self-esteem. While the concept of group-esteem comes with all of the wisdom of a fourteen-year-old, there really is something to be said about this approach. We have to learn how to esteem ourselves and not look for it to come from others, especially the men we meet.

When you project a small sense of self-worth with little value, that is what you are going to attract. Because you draw unto yourself as you are, what will come to you will not be good for you. For instance, if you present yourself as a rock or a pebble, worthy of very little, that is what you will receive, very little. But when you have gone through your process and have come out like pure gold, then you have to command the confidence that comes with the value of precious worth. As a child of the Most High God, you must let that status become a part of the space you occupy and let it reflect in your presence. As you begin attracting to yourself what you are, there will be someone worthy of all that you are.

As you are working from within and your confidence and self-esteem are commensurate with your wonderful you, this is a great time to consider how well you have learned to love yourself. I have seen many of my coaching clients who never really understood the meaning of self-love. This does not suggest being obnoxious or arrogant but simply practicing one of the many things God has commanded us to do. In the book of Matthew we are directed to love our neighbor as we love ourselves. Of course, in context we are to treat others well, but we cannot overlook the inherent and implied command of loving one's self.

I believe if we were not intended to love ourselves then perhaps we would have been instructed in scripture to love our neighbor the way we love "Mama and them." In all sincerity, however, you are never going to be able to give what you don't have. How would you ever be able to share love for someone else if you don't have love for yourself? You cannot. You have to fully embrace the idea of loving yourself unconditionally before you would ever be able to do the same in any type of relationship.

Part of loving yourself is learning that service does not equal sacrifice, and just because we are of service to others does not mean we have to sacrifice ourselves. Martyrdom isn't attractive in a suicide bomber and it isn't attractive in a woman of worth. I have coached women who are not able to say no. Some simply design their personal boundaries in such a way that their wants and desires are constantly compromised. When these tendencies exist in our natural state, they tend to become enhanced when we enter into a relationship. If you identify this as something you need to improve upon, start noticing the subtle ways in which you are not able to say no and must constantly accommodate others. I tell my coaching clients that they need to work on their assertiveness skills to develop boundaries and limitations with the ability to say "no" as needed.

Several years ago two of my friends and I rented a beach home for a get away with our sons. While we were at the beach during the spring break, we realized that a teammate from our son's sports team was also there with his mother, Pam. Now, Pam tends to be a bit self-absorbed, but usually we tolerate her because our boys enjoy playing together. My friends and I had spent the day entertaining the boys, playing on the beach, stocking the house with food, cooking, and had finally come home to our time for rest and relaxation. After a very full and exhausting day, we were lounging around preparing to unwind for the evening and watch a movie we had rented.

Pam comes to our house, after she has spent her time at a day spa, notices that we are relaxing but proceeds to request that one of us accompany her to the store to pick up a few grocery items for her house. I immediately declined, stating the obvious that after the long day I just had, there wasn't any energy or desire to go shopping. One of my friends, Samantha, also declined for the same reason. Lynn, on the other hand, is the perpetual people pleaser. She was the most adamant in the group about relaxing for the remainder of the evening, and yet she sacrificed her wishes in order to accompany Pam to the store.

Upon Lynn's return, she lamented how tired she was and how miserable she felt having to shop after such a long day. I spent quite a bit of time during the remainder of the trip trying to help Lynn identify why she felt the need to constantly sacrifice what was important to her in order to accommodate someone else, to understand that kindness and courtesy can only go as far as they are extended, and to accept a balance between walking in love and walking to be taken advantage of. Pam did not show any consideration in her asking someone to go shopping with her at a late hour. Lynn should not have felt obligated to put herself on the altar of sacrifice.

Lynn needed some work with assertiveness and the ability to make decisions that are as healthy for her as they are for the person making the request. When a request is out of your space of reasonable service, learn that loving yourself is not optional and you are entitled to establish personal boundaries. You must be able to love yourself before you could ever move forward and show love in your relationships. Without personal direction and boundaries, you will lose yourself and become needful of a serious navigational intervention to get you back on course. Before getting lost in this area, remember it is okay to stop and ask for directions to your destination.

CHAPTER 5

Okay by Yourself- Unplug the Life Support

At this point in your reading, I pray that at a minimum level of understanding, you know that your substance and worth are not connected to a man or to giving birth. I would like to reiterate the necessity of being comfortable with your individuality. Try this exercise: on a piece of paper write down the numbers 1 through 9. Notice that the number one (1) is a whole number. It has no breaks, divisions or attachments. It is completion in and of itself. Other numbers have breaks, turns or angles, but the number one is complete without anything else. Well, the same concept should be applied to our lives: we are living examples of our own completion.

I often wonder how the Bible tells us that two shall become one and everybody focuses on the two people coming together. The implication is that there are two people to begin with. Scripture does not make allowance for one half of a person to come together or three fourths of a person to come together. Instead it is clear that two completely whole individuals will come together and create a union.

Presume that you are a thirty-five-year-old professional who has never been married and doesn't have any children. Do you honestly believe that you have not and cannot contribute to the world because you are not married with children? When a sense of incompleteness for not having a man in your life begins to take over, what you are telling the world is that the thirty-five years of being your wonderful self are nothing more than a waste of a creation. Not even the best of what any man has to offer can create and determine your worth. How can a man come along and make you who and what you already are?

Consider the talent and skill of any great athlete; a coach coming into her life doesn't make her an athlete. She is already an athlete before the coach ever comes into her life. The coach just brings out the best in the athlete but the coach does not make the athlete. The same is true from the perspective of desiring a mate; you just want someone who helps bring out the best of what already exists within you. For some women, instead of seeking a relationship for the purposes of enhancing their lives, the need for a mate has become their life support system.

Ladies, it is time to unplug the life support systems that have convinced us that a mate is the only thing that can sustain us. Through my coaching, I have seen what I consider the addiction of needing a mate with a pull so strong that it has women compromising themselves more than any drug habit ever could. Abandonment of perspective, lying to friends and family, promiscuity, fiscal mismanagement, all of the things we know in the context of drug or alcohol abuse, are also readily apparent when women are suffering from mate addiction. I have met and coached women who have departed from any level of common sense to adopt all of the characteristics of an addict doing whatever is necessary for that next mate fix.

It is absolutely necessary to understand that a mate cannot be the solution to whatever you believe is the problem. If you are wandering through life depressed, unhappy, and feeling incomplete, what would happen if you invited a mate into your life? You would be depressed, unhappy, and feeling incomplete with someone else around to make his life as miserable as yours. People do not make a change until they recognize the need and then they act upon it. Until you make a change in you, all that will ever happen when you enter a relationship is a continuation of everything about you that was problematic prior to the inception of the relationship, only doubled.

Please understand that part of the overdrive for some women to have a mate comes from societal influences that have us so convinced that we must marry and procreate for our lives to take on true meaning. In previous chapters, we have covered ways to not let such influences consume us. It bears repeating, though, that we must have our who and why so firmly established that we do not take on the burden of what others think we need for our lives. Imagine how much easier your life would be if you had to think only about what God thinks of your life.

To explore this issue further, let's use Condoleezza Rice as our example of what society suggests in this regard. Whether you agree with her politics or not, the one thing that cannot be disputed is that she is a very intelligent and highly educated woman.

Ms. Rice occupies one of the most commanding positions in the government of the most powerful country in the world, yet there is still a sense of sympathy for her because she is single. I have heard talk show hosts and news commentators make reference to her single status as though it is an area of her life where she has not been able to succeed.

Even recently in the news there was some scuttlebutt about her not having any children. I don't know Ms. Rice personally so I cannot speak for her. I am aware enough to consider that perhaps being single is a choice that she welcomes in her life. Imagine for a moment that Ms. Rice is happy and content with the choices she has made regarding her career and her personal life. Is it possible that she does not agonize over her single status but instead embraces who she is as an individual and what she has purposed to do with her life? Of course it is highly possible and even probable. I would venture to say that society focuses on Ms. Rice's single-hood more than she does.

I have a very good friend, Victoria, who is thirty-nine and single without any children. Victoria has a wonderful career. She is active in her local church and has traveled the world on several missionary trips. She embodies self-confidence and contentment with her very full and busy life. I have often asked Victoria how she is able to manage her single status without feeling like it is her personal scarlet letter to be worn with shame. Her position is that, while she doesn't always want to be alone, she does not let the mere thought of loneliness consume her. Several months ago when I spoke with Victoria about being single and almost forty, I suggested to her that I believe sometimes our thoughts are worse than our reality.

We may think about being a certain age with no mate and no children, but the thought of it is worse than actually living it. Victoria completely agreed with me because she has often wondered how she would have ever balanced her career and her missionary trips with a family. Since Victoria finds her experiences invaluable, she knows that she is actually enjoying her life as it is, for the moment, and to think that she should have something that she does not have would be counterproductive. I have helped many women I've coached realize that when they think about God, their blessings, and the life they do have, the thoughts of being without a mate are not nearly as negative.

In reality, these women actually have a good life and the thought of what isn't should not overshadow thoughts of what is. I contend that when you are living life with confidence and purpose, while trusting God with your ultimate destiny, you know that He will give you the desires of your heart. If it is truly your heart's desire, the right person for you will come along when the time is right so until your then, enjoy the journey as you wait for your when. Remember the Apostle Paul's teaching-it is good for us to learn how to be content with where we are. If God has you single in this season, learn to trust His plan for your life. Perhaps there are other things you need to focus on, and a relationship is nothing more than a distraction from where God desires your attention. Wants are always more special than needs.

Why not want a mate but not need a mate? When I was a young girl, I had a difficult time mastering the concept of wants versus needs. I would tell my mother, with all of the drama of an Academy Award winning actress, that I needed something. It was usually a new outfit, some jewelry, or some other extra accoutrement for my life. My mother would always respond with two comments: One, I was old enough for my wants not to hurt me and two, I needed to learn the difference between wants and needs. Certainly there are times as adults when we still wrestle with the difference between wants and needs.

There are some of us who could use a real refresher course in the difference. I have come to see wants as those things that would be nice to invite into my life, but do not alter my ability to exist if I don't have them. Obviously water, food, shelter and clothing provide the most basic of our needs and we can build upon life from there. But life becomes more colorful and interesting when we can begin to add the upgrade items to the basics: A nice house, designer shoes, multiple clothing articles, jewelry, and luxury cars. When we are able to shift our perspective and see the possibility of a mate as an add-on upgrade, then we have taken the relationship concept to an entirely different level. Instead of believing we need someone in our life, it is so much better to want them.

If we truly believe we need a mate in order to exist, we will become anxious about our situation and often act out of character. But if we are comfortable with the concept of wanting a mate, just as we want other things that fulfill our life more, this attitude will help eliminate the sense of desperation we sometimes project to men. Just as we know that jewelry or designer shoes are things we may want, in our rational mind we must know that our living, breathing existence is not sustained by these things. And so it is with a mate. We may want one, but our living, breathing existence is not sustained by a mate.

Neediness cannot and will not foster a good relationship, so you must learn to be okay by yourself. In my opinion, while most men are potentially flattered initially, they do not respond well, over time, to neediness. Unfortunately, what makes matters worse is that the wrong men have the right radar for needy women. Men with pathetic, at best, demographics are always able to find the women who are needy enough to put up with just about anything. Everyone knows of or has heard of at least one "Snookie." This is the guy who is over 35 years old, lives at home with his mother, has a few children by multiple baby mamas, justifies his lack of paying any child support because the baby mama would spend the money on herself, and considers employment an undesirable option.

Snookie is always able to find and detect a needy woman. Maybe you can identify with the woman who will give him a cell phone and put him on her cellular plan because she can never get in touch with him. Or the woman who has no problem picking up the tab at the restaurant because Snookie forgot his wallet, or he is waiting for his income tax refund. And, of course there's the woman who will let Snookie move into her home because his mother is always nagging him because she doesn't understand him. Snookie's radar is sharp-shooter accurate for these needy women who will basically endure any and everything just because of their need to have a man. With situations like this one, it is best understood in the context of choices we make.

Please know that there is a direct correlation between the decisions you make and the quality of man you have, or don't have, in your life. Instead of pitching a tent and setting up camp in the victimized state of your choices, why not begin to make better decisions with your dating life and hold yourself accountable?

Have you ever wondered why some women have never been married and yet others with the exact same demographics are working on husband number two or three? My experience has shown that one of the major differences is that women who have married multiple times do not project the sense of needing to be married. Because they are complete and self-contained, these women are able to adopt a been-there, done-that attitude with no room for neediness. There is a strong sense of self that clearly demonstrates the ability to be okay, with or without the relationship.

Choosing a relationship is far more flattering to a man because you are telling him he was a choice and not a need. If needs speak to the basics, what you are saying is that he was special enough to be an upgraded add-on choice in your life. If you have a tendency towards acting needy, this behavior should be addressed. Realize that activity and involvement are good solutions for neediness. The old saying that an idle mind is the devils workshop is very true as it applies to projecting neediness. If you have too much time available to obsess over what a man is or isn't doing in your life, then you need a time allocation makeover. When you are actively improving yourself spiritually, mentally, physically, and financially, you shouldn't have much time to call a man that you just met five times a day. Instead you are in preparation for becoming the best you possible and do not want to spend time and energy obsessing over every man you meet.

CHAPTER 6

What's in Your Trunk?

As you are preparing for your journey, consider what you have in your trunk. I have learned that one of the more critical mistakes women make is to drag the past around like a giant albatross around their neck. Please know however, that as a professionally trained Life Coach, I am well aware that there are women who have experienced horrific things in their past that relate to abuse or other tragedies. If this is something you are struggling with in any way, then I encourage you to seek professional Christian counseling to identify the issue and work through it.

This chapter speaks only to those occurrences in the past that are now simply a matter of fact, not a matter of life-altering events that have you paralyzed and unable to function. Certainly we are all byproducts of life experiences that have helped to shape and mold us into who we are at present. From the moment we were born, certain events would determine how we thought and reacted to everything we experienced. This is all part of the process that makes us so wonderfully unique because we all have different people, places and events that deposited something into our lives, albeit good or bad.

I believe that for most of us, our problem is not knowing how to take what happened, learn from the experience, and then move on. Yet another one of my favorite inspirational scriptures is found in Philippians 3:13." But one thing I do: Forgetting what is behind and straining toward what is ahead "There are various times in my life when this scripture really ministered to my heart. It gave me permission not to agonize over the fact that even if l didn't have it all together yet, the one thing I could do was let go of what had already happened and look toward the future.

This was a concept I could embrace to the fullest because, while I couldn't change my yesterday, I could impact my tomorrow. After all, like most people who have lived more than a minute or two, I have regrets about some of my choices both passive and active. The former being mistakes I made by doing nothing, and the latter being mistakes I made by taking the wrong action. What makes the difference for me is accepting that I could not let whatever happened in the past become a negative influence and potentially derail my destiny. I had to learn that, in order to walk effectively in the vision God had for my life, I had to remain facing forward. Now, I do not in any way endorse forgetting about your past as if it never happened. Oftentimes there are lessons to be learned from whatever our personal history has been, and if we simply forget, then we have lost the value of the past experience(s). Instead, we must learn from it, grow with it and ultimately move on which is not synonymous with forgetting.

Lorraine was one of my coaching clients who struggled with not knowing how to let go of the past. When I first started working with Lorraine she was 34 years old and divorced after a very brief marriage right out of high school that did not result in any children. Lorraine was a flight attendant, a career she loved because of her passion to travel. When she wasn't working, Lorraine would go to the most exotic places on earth and just enjoy the beauty of God's creation. Lorraine is very outgoing, meets a great number of people in her travels and she regularly receives invitations for all types of social events.

When Lorraine and I first met, I also met head-on with her inability to let go of what I refer to as the insignificant to-the-now-events from her past. For approximately one year, Lorraine dated a guy who she believed to be a very caring, honest and trustworthy man. She believed they were dating each other exclusively and had begun to consider the possibility that maybe one day they would get married. Unfortunately, Lorraine discovered that her guy was lying to her regarding his idea of exclusive dating. He was actually seeing other people the entire time he was dating Lorraine. This discovery left Lorraine no less than devastated. We can all imagine that for a time, after the deception and break-up, Lorraine remained very emotionally upset, which is understandable behavior that would be expected. However, Lorraine was still reaping the harvest of this rotten seed two years after it was planted.

She had become so distrusting of men that, whenever she did go on a date, she presented herself as a paranoid employee of the Female Bureau of Investigation. Lorraine would describe dates that sounded like nothing short of an interrogation from America's most wanted.

Lorraine needed to learn from her experience, grow with it, and then move on. Yes, she had a bad experience with that particular man, but it did not give her license to prosecute every man she would ever date for a crime committed by someone else. Lorraine was causing more havoc in her personal life than her ex-boyfriend had. What her ex had done was a moment in time; she was the one who was making it a lifetime. Because of one event, Lorraine projected as a bitter woman, which is unattractive at best. When you have a spirit of bitterness you become ineffective for the kingdom and miserable for those around you. Fortunately for Lorraine, she eventually learned how to let go and get on with life in a positive way. After all, she should consider herself blessed and highly favored because she could have married the guy, purchased a home with him, had a few children and then found out he was lying and dating other women the entire time.

In actuality he did her a favor to show himself as unworthy of her time, trust, and attention. This was a lesson and a blessing, and instead of holding on to anger and resentment, she should have sent him a nice thank you note. Ask yourself what insignificant-to-the-now experiences are you allowing to make you bitter. When events from the past are insignificant to your present reality, isn't it time to let them go? Consider the serenity prayer that asks God to grant you the serenity to accept the things that you cannot change. Once you accept the past as an unchangeable learning lesson, you have the freedom to move positively into the present.

What I want you to do is to clean out your trunk so that you have room for new experiences and blessings for your journey. As long as your trunk is overflowing with old, insignificant items you don't need anymore, you won't be able to put anything new and significant inside. Surely if God is willing to cast our sin into the depths of the sea, we can let go of a past experience and move on.

CHAPTER 7

Are Your Ready for the Journey?

As you begin to consider inviting a real relationship into your life, please consider if you are ready for the journey or not. I am a very systematic, methodical, and organized person who abhors the idea of not being prepared for whatever comes my way that could negatively impact my creature comforts. Whenever I am embarking on a road trip, even if only a short distance, I am well prepared. I have everything in my car from a first-aid kit to a toiletry kit, equipped with make-up, insect repellant, and anything else to make sure I am ready, come what may. Just as you would prepare for a road trip, so it is with the preparation before entertaining a potential relationship. Begin to think about your own personal state of affairs. At this point in the reading you should be firmly rooted and secure within yourself; you have a vision and you are living on purpose.

Now is the time to ask yourself the question, what does your fruit look like? The Bible tells us that it is for God's glory that we bear much good fruit. If a fruit inspector were to suddenly show up and examine your fruit, would he see a basket that is overflowing with a great harvest of fruit just ripe for the picking or, a scarce crop with bruised and damaged fruit covered in brown spots or fruit that has been sitting so long it is rotten? Your life and all that you are accomplishing is an open testimony to what you will invite into your life by way of a relationship. If your life reflects low levels of production with a bruised and rotten product, then you will attract a low level, bruised, rotten man. So before you attract what you positively don't want, why not take some time to work on yourself? Ask yourself the following questions:

- Do I have a career that I love?
- What would happen if I turned my career into a business for myself?
- Am I working a job just to get by?
- If I am working just to make it, what am I doing to make a change?
- Is God enlarging my territory? If not, why?
- Am I living beyond my means?
- Do I own my own home?
- Have I considered home ownership?
- How is my credit?
- Am I swimming in debt?
- Do I regularly save a portion of my income?
- How am I constantly improving my personal development?
- When was the last time I took a class to further my knowledge?
- How am I expanding my horizons?

» Do I read anything not found in a rack at the super market checkout?

The answers to these questions should cause you to take your own pulse on how prepared you are to meet all that God has for you. Please remember that Cinderella was nothing more than a fairy tale; in the real world you have to prepare for who and what you want. You cannot sit around depressed, in a dead-end job, living in an apartment you have rented for more than five years with no purpose or vision, with no plans for change or improvement and still think that your prince charming is coming on his white horse to take you away to his castle. That only happens in the land of make-believe. Instead, if you are just living day-to-day without any vision, any plans, or any consideration towards self-improvement, your prince charming is going to come get you on public transportation and take you back to his mama's house.

A good, godly man is not going to find it appealing to

set up residency in your raggedy dead-end world. It would behoove you to begin developing yourself to the level at which you want to attract. The more you know and are able to participate in or discuss, the greater your circle of potential becomes. When all you do is go back and forth to work on the subway and then come home to sit on your sofa with a box of bonbons to watch repeats of the Jerry Springer show, the level to which you can interact and be interesting is very limited. If you did meet a really nice person, what are you going to offer in the way of substance that can sustain any real interest? But when you participate in several hobbies, are actively involved in self-development, and have interesting experiences and knowledge from which to draw, you are able to attract and sustain from a much greater selection of potential candidates.

There are some basic steps you can take that will make you feel more accomplished and give you opportunities to expand your horizons, meet new people, and contribute something worthwhile to the world. There are classes at community schools, at local churches, and at the university level that can increase your knowledge base in everything from biblical studies to Thai cooking. Maybe you have always wanted to be fluent in a foreign language. Go ahead and learn a particular craft or strive to know more about different cultures in other countries. These are all the types of things you could study that would enhance your personal being. If you don't already, you might also consider learning how to golf or play tennis. It's easily accessible at most local community centers. Even the person operating with the most limited funds has access to personal development via the public library and the internet; another set of tools that can help you begin learning and growing. In fact, reading is the great equalizer because for anything you are unable to experience first-hand, due to the constraints of time and money, you can at least know vicariously through the written word.

Once you invest enough time in learning about something and your interest is sufficiently piqued, you will begin to focus on allocating the necessary resources for a first-hand experience. For example, if you begin to read books about French culture and start to dine at fine French restaurants and shop in European-style boutiques and love it, eventually you will want to travel to Paris and experience it for yourself. Step away from the confines of I-could-never and begin to ask yourself, why not me? Remember, it is only when you begin to walk with expectancy that things begin to happen.

CHAPTER 8

Is Your Vehicle Well Maintained for the Trip?

The Temple, our body, has to be right! We must be fit and healthy in order to receive all that God has for us; it is our reasonable act of worship. As we search to hear from God and understand what God has for us, we must be in a place where we can hear from Him. We want powerful careers, we want to be excellent wives and mothers, we want to be of service to mankind and make a difference in this world. Some of us want to be useful in various ministries, and then some of us want to be all of these things. Yet if we willfully destroy that which God has trusted us with how will He trust us with more? Have you ever considered that a component of marriage and motherhood consists of caring for others, yet you can't even take care of yourself the way God intended? Our destiny is disrupted by our own self-destructive behaviors and we must begin taking ownership of a new and improved stewardship of our Temple.

I cannot stress to you enough how much exercise, eating right, and generally taking care of you is tantamount to loving yourself and demonstrating godly principles. I am a firm believer in what I have named my "D5" model which plainly states that developing discipline and determination will decide your destiny. The area of self-care demonstrates how true this statement is. When you are determined to develop the discipline to eat right, exercise, drink water, and get enough rest, health and fitness will be your destiny. Once you are practicing the D5 model of self-care, the good habits you reinforce will make you so much more effective in other areas of your life, and most importantly the discipline will make you a better disciple for the Kingdom. As a result, your destiny will become a place you want to go versus a place where you arrive by default.

For women who have not had the opportunity to peek inside the mind of a man, trust someone who grew up in a predominantly male village-men are visual. I know it is hard for some women to accept this as truth, but there isn't any way around this physiological aspect of a man. While most women would agree they want to be valued for who they are on the inside, unfortunately it takes most men a minute to discover the inside because they must first find something attractive on the outside. When we present ourselves with no regard to self-care, it just doesn't work for the male gender. They need to look and see something interesting in order to take the time to open the package. There is something about a woman who takes care of herself; it shows to the rest of the world. When you are fit and healthy, that is easily identifiable.

Health and fitness also reinforce the premise that you care about treating yourself right and you will not tolerate anything less from him. Is this to imply that we all have to present the perfect size 8, Beyoncé like appearance? Of course not. But who are you really fooling when you boldly proclaim, "A man has to love me just like I am?" This just doesn't work when you look like you don't love yourself, so how would you ever expect someone else to come along and love you? If I illustrate this in the context of looking to purchase a home on a cold rainy day, picture the following: House number one has a raggedy dirt yard in the front, the roof is in need of repair, the concrete in the driveway is all cracked and chipped and some of the front windows are broken out.

House number two has a beautiful flower bed in the front, the roof is in good condition, all the maintenance on the home has been completed, including a new paint job, and the windows all have nice curtains. In an instant, human nature will have us making a judgment call about the two houses even before we see the inside. Both houses could look exactly the same on the inside, or the one that is well maintained on the outside may be a disaster when you get inside or vice versa. House number one does not motivate you to get out of the car to endure the cold and rain to see what the inside of the house looks like, but house number two at least motivates you to see what is inside because it reflects potential. Regardless, the impression has already been made about the two different houses before you even see the inside.

Granted, once you purchase the home you will spend 99 percent of your time focusing on the inside of the home, but the initial visual slanted your thoughts of the home. I assure you, men are that way when they see a woman; they can't help but make a judgment based on what they initially see.

This doesn't mean that throughout the relationship they won't end up spending 99 percent of the time loving what's on the inside, but first there certainly has to be something inviting enough on the outside that speaks to the potential of your inside. Ask yourself what is speaking to your potential? From a man's perspective, dating can be like getting out of the car on a cold, rainy day. The potential for drama and the fear of rejection are valid concerns for men. Therefore, if there isn't anything inviting and interesting on the outside, it just seems easier to stay inside where it is warm and dry.

Amber is one of my coaching clients that I had to spend an enormous amount of time with trying to help her grasp the truth of this concept. She is 37 years old, has never married, has no children, owns her condo, and works as a nurse in a very busy hospital. When I first began working with Amber, it was obvious to me that from the neck up she was still partial to her Marcia Brady straight hair and plain Jane look. Not that there was anything wrong with how Marcia looked as a teenager in a 1970's sitcom, but for a grown woman in 2007 for purposes of dating readiness, it was just not working. Refusing to wear any make-up or to maintain a good skin care regimen began to detract from Amber's look, especially as she approached 40 years old.

Additionally, Amber maintained a steady diet of Krispy Kreme donuts and diet soda which directly reflected in her overall appearance of health and wellness. Because she worked long hours, had poor eating habits and no exercise, she always look tired and worn down. Add to this the fact that Amber is 5'2" and at her heaviest weight she was slightly over 225 pounds; it was plain to see that Amber was in need of a radical renovation. Fortunately for her, Amber realized she needed to do something different and that is when she began her coaching sessions.

For those of you, who are still sitting comfortably in the false reality of loving me for me, please know that Amber has a wonderful personality with a great sense of humor and a very caring attitude, hence her decision to become a nurse. She also had zero dating prospects in the present and none on the horizon. Amber portrayed to the world self-debasement; there was nothing about her appearance to indicate that she valued herself and expected others to do the same. Of course, working in the health care industry only made matters worse because anybody she came in contact with, in a professional environment, knew that she should realize the importance of maintaining good health.

Amber was adamant that when the right man came along he would love her for the beautiful, caring person she is on the inside and she shouldn't have to change her look for anybody. While Amber is correct in that she should not have to change her look to please somebody else, she should still want to be her personal best and project that personal best, not for anyone else, but because she values herself. Even if it was unintentional, the persona that Amber took forth into the world and into her relationships was one of, "I don't care and you shouldn't either."

Eventually, Amber began to realize that she had to do something different, so she began really putting an emphasis on her own self-care. One year after coaching, Amber has lost 75 pounds; she regularly works out, has changed her eating habits, and has embraced an entirely different look. She not only has more energy, she feels better, too. The person she projects to the world is one of health and vitality now. Amber is now able to demonstrate that she is a priority and would expect the same in a relationship. Dating options have increased for Amber and she has an overall sense of well-being. While Amber is not a Beyoncé look-alike, size 8, she is comfortable in her skin and the ability to maintain a healthy weight for her body type, not an image that Hollywood or the supermarket tabloids dictate.

You see, it is less about her dress size and more about an overall feeling of well-being that she now projects. Now that Amber has an exterior that is well maintained, men are able to consider the potential of a connection with her inner traits. While Amber is still the same person on the inside, she is now able to create enough interest for a man to get out of the car and endure the cold and rain to see what the inside of the house is like.

CHAPTER 9

What to Know Before You Go

I have met many women who can bring out an entire laundry list of what they want in a mate. Everything from a physical description of their ideal to how much money he makes annually is spelled out chapter and verse. While it is excellent to understand some of the things that you desire in your potential mate, most women overlook the importance of identifying what you don't want in a mate. Consider that you are going on a major shopping spree where money is not an object. You would eliminate shopping at certain stores just based on the fact that they sell items you don't want to buy. If your idea of roughing it is a hotel without 24-hour room service, chances are you need not begin your shopping spree in a store that sells camping goods.

Knowing all that before you arrive at the mall will save you wasted time in a store with no potential for purchase. Often, women are not even remotely able to articulate what characteristics they do not want. When my coaching clients tell me they are very confident in knowing everything they want out of a relationship, I will usually flip the script and ask them what they don't want in a relationship. This is the point where most clients will find themselves dumbfounded. For as much thought as they put into knowing everything they are looking for in a mate, they have not even considered what they don't want. Consider that, during the dating phase, what was once deemed slightly annoying becomes magnified ten times over in a long-term relationship. As you see potential behavioral red flags during the dating phase, please be aware that the behavior will not miraculously disappear as the relationship continues.

One of my coaching clients, Alexis, was able to clearly articulate exactly what she wanted in a man. She was specific regarding education, profession, salary range, and spiritual orientation. Alexis met a man who met all of the qualifications she was seeking and they began dating. Although she noticed that he seemed a bit fanatical about football, she didn't give it much thought. During the initial dates the guy Alexis was dating would always incorporate football into their outings . He always made sure they were near a television during all of their dates, even if they had to go to a sports bar, just to make sure he did not miss a game.

Initially Alexis thought this to be just mildly annoying, not anything to be concerned with. After a few months of dating, Alexis wanted her guy to meet some of her friends, so she accepted a dinner invitation at the home of one of her dear friends. As fate would have it, there was a football game on television during the night of the dinner. Alexis' guy spent the entire evening glued to the television and even asked to take his dinner to the room where a wide screen television was. He was perfectly comfortable not interacting with the rest of the dinner guests while he sat and watched the football game.

Even though Alexis and her friends were trying to include him in the evening, he declined any conversation for the sake of the game. After dinner, on the way home, Alexis confronted her guy to let him know how upset she was with his incredible rudeness towards her friends. She could not believe that he would ignore everyone all evening just to watch a football game. Interestingly enough, he did not appreciate her making such a big deal over his not talking to her friends during dinner. His expectation was that everyone should have understood the fact that one of his favorite teams was playing that evening.

This is a case of the slightly annoying becoming magnified with time. After just a few short months Alexis became bothered by a behavior that was there all along; the magnification process had already begun. Fortunately, as Alexis discussed this situation with me as her coach, she was able to recognize that this was not a good match for her. Looking at a long-term relationship with a man who was more committed to football than he could ever be to her, or the things that she valued, was not the direction she wanted to go for the long haul of life. Alexis can now identify that sports fanaticism is a quality she does not want in a potential mate.

Begin to think about your past experiences and start compiling a list of the things that you do not want in a potential mate. This is actually more difficult than you may think. It is easy to think positively about those things that we are hopeful about, but thinking in terms of what may seem to take us further away from having that someone special in our life is far more challenging. You are basically creating the ground rules for your life by defining what would constitute a forfeiture of the game.

Imagine if you met a man who really cared about you and wanted to please you. If you were able to specifically point out to him everything you don't want and behaviors that you don't like or appreciate, his job would be that much easier. Consider making this list a step towards setting your relationship up for success and not letting it drift towards failure due to his not knowing what you don't like, and you, quite frankly not knowing either.

CHAPTER 10

Strike Gold along the Way

Now that you have a better understanding about what you don't want, it will be easier for you to consider some of the characteristics you would like to have in a potential mate. In our society, we have become conditioned to think of the term "gold-digger" as a negative description for a woman who is looking to date and ultimately marry only a man with money. I recently saw a television news show that did a story on a company that offers a new form of speed dating. The general premise of this company is to connect very attractive women with very wealthy men. In order to participate, the women must submit five photos of themselves to be judged by a panel of experts, and the men must submit documentation substantiating a net worth of at least several million dollars. Once approved, the participants are invited to a cocktail party at an upscale establishment in a major city.

The news show had cameras at one of the cocktail parties, and both men and women alike were more than willing to not only be seen on camera, but to answer questions from the news reporter. The general consensus among the participants was that most men want a really good looking woman and most women want a rich man. Watching this news program would have you believe the state of dating is just that grim. Of course, we have to factor in that this show demonstrated a room full of people with the same common shallow denominator. That would reasonably explain why everyone interviewed on camera believed what they were doing made perfect sense.

I have hope that there are still many singles who are able to see other facets in the dating selection process aside from just physical beauty or mere net worth. There are many other variables that should be considered in a possible mate, and for women specifically, their decisions should not be solely based on money. The key differentiator is potential. Where you meet a man in his present state is not nearly as important as where his potential is going to take him for his future. Investigate his vision and his plan of execution to see where his destiny is leading him. Since you are now living by the D5 model, you can notice how well Mr. Potential is living with discipline and determination, which are great indicators of what he is really all about.

Perhaps I should let you in on a secret; there are ways to strike gold without having to dig for it. Just be aware that, contrary to popular belief, finding a man of gold is not merely dependent on the size of his bank account. "Gold" in this context is simply a metaphor for a man of great worth in the areas that are critical for sustaining a lasting, fulfilling, and meaningful relationship. A man of great worth is a godly man who is going to want the best for you at all times. He is going to understand the importance of respect, trust, and honesty. A man of great worth will realize that you will sometimes have completely different thoughts and needs than he does, but he will honor those differences and support what is important to you.

This would be a great time to consider what qualities you want in a potential mate. Actually take the time to make a list of the qualities that are non-negotiable versus what would be nice to have. For example, you will want to stand strong in your faith and not be unequally yoked. You are keenly aware that a man who is not a Christian is unacceptable for you. Let's say you love to work the crossword puzzle section of the New York Times, it would be great if you found someone who shared that same interest, but it is okay if they do not.

I like to summarize what to look for in a man with three things: They have to love the Lord, they have to love their mother, and they can't be cheap. The rationale for what seems very simplistic is that loving God gives them the biblical guidelines to be a good husband and father. Loving their mother shows their respect and reverence for women. If they can't love the woman who gave them life, they wouldn't do well by you either, especially if you had plans on becoming the mother of his children. Being cheap is a negative and problematic mindset as well as an action. To be practical and budget minded is fine, but cheapness is a red flag for other issues; the most important one being that a cheap man will not see the real value in you.

As you begin to make your list, pretend you are catalog shopping and you are able to pick out exactly what you want. It doesn't mean you can only accept exactly what you picked, but it will certainly give you a frame of reference to consider. If you are struggling with this exercise, go back to your list of what you do not want and think of the polar opposite to that trait. For example, if you don't want someone who is an unhealthy couch potato, you can put 'active' and 'fit' on your preferred list of qualities for your potential partner. I can't stress enough the importance of knowing what you don't want in a mate as well as knowing what you do want. This awareness will prevent you from wasting time and energy in situations that, over time, aren't going anywhere that you would be interested in visiting. Remember, it is always okay to stop and get directions for your destiny.

CHAPTER 11

Why Are You Going There?

Have you ever been going along on your way and wondered why you are even going in that direction? You aren't happy with the condition of your relationships and yet you continue doing the same thing you have always done, going to the same places you have always gone, and just waiting for something different to happen. This is insanity at its best. I mean, have you ever stopped to ask yourself why you are going there? You may be participating in a negative relationship where you are not honored or respected. Understand that people will only treat you the way you allow them to treat you. Don't be foolish about the relationships you find yourself in and stop wasting time reinforcing poor behavior. Most men who act like jerks have developed this pattern of unacceptable behavior over a period of time.

When we as women continue to tolerate being treated poorly or less-than, all we are doing is enabling a man to continue along the path of mistreatment. They will continue either to treat you poorly or move on to the next woman to continue in the same unacceptable manner. We are all products of behavior that has either worked for us in the past or has been corrected over time. If a man is selfish and you foster that behavior by continuing to sacrifice your wants and needs in order to accommodate the relationship, do you really think he is going to one day decide to change his ways? Of course not. This man will continue along on the path of selfishness for the rest of his life or until he meets a woman who stops him in his tracks, draws the line in the sand, and says, "No! I will not accept this from you."

Now that you know what you know, isn't it time for you to be the one to draw the line in the sand and say no? Isn't it time to make sure we value ourselves more than we value having a relationship just for the sake of having one? What is the real purpose in having a man in your life who doesn't bring anything of value and substance into your life? When you are the sole giver and he is the sole taker, the relationship is out of balance, and unbalanced relationships cannot be sustained for any significant length of time without your becoming miserable and possibly even bitter along the way. Don't set yourself up for this type of failure.

One evening at a birthday party with my husband and some friends, I met Bob, who had gone to college with one of my husband's friends. Because I am always doing research, I never miss a chance to discover information for a better understanding of relationship dynamics. I noticed that Bob, a surgeon with a wife and two children, was very flirtatious with women in the club, buying them drinks and engaging in pick-up-like behavior. Bob was wearing a wedding band, yet the women were accepting the drinks, and a few were willing to give him their phone number.

I overheard Bob telling one young, overly impressed woman that he would be available only on Thursday evenings because on Wednesday nights he had Bible study and on Friday nights his son had pee wee football. I am not a naive prude, and I am aware that there are people who engage in extramarital affairs, but this approach shocked me. When most roamers go out, they take off their wedding bands and make a pretense of being single. Here was Bob, however, being forthright about his family status right from the beginning. Of course, much to my husband's dismay, because sometimes even he can't believe that I have the audacity to ask such bold questions, I asked Bob how he was able to have on a wedding ring and openly attempt to date. The long and short of Bob's answer was because the women allowed it. How incredibly sad for the women who have given Bob license for his ill behavior.

While we cannot take ownership for Bob's lack of respect towards his marriage, as women we must realize our role in perpetuating the type of behavior Bob displayed. If Bob were told no each time he began his little flirt game and women did not accept his offers, eventually there would be no reward for his inappropriate behavior. Or at least the approach would have to change. Not that I condone a man who will lie and pretend to a woman that he is single, but at the very least until the woman discovers he is married she has not compromised her integrity and dignity from the start. When a man meets you and he is married, for you to accept his advances, be it for dating or ongoing conversation, you have already told him that it is okay for him not to respect you because you don't respect yourself.

Even the most outrageous behaviors and habits

can become commonplace if they are allowed to continue for a long period of time. If you find yourself constantly interacting and relating to men who do not respect you, eventually this will become normal and you will begin to accept it as such. Regardless of what shape and form the lack of regard and respect takes, you cannot let it continue to the point that it becomes the norm for you. It is time to take your pride and self-worth out of the drawer of desperation so you can boldly proclaim to the world that, "If you are not going to approach me correctly, then I am not the one!" We are byproducts of our choices. Changing your decisions can change your destiny. Just remember, it is okay to stop and get directions on the way to your destination.

CHAPTER 12

Does That Car Look Like It Will Make the Trip?

Yes, that certain height and weight; that preferred hair color or hair texture. Indeed, women have their preferences, and they can be stuck in patterns that are strictly followed, very much like a map. Of course, the better pattern to follow would be not only what you are attracting but also what you are looking for. One of my coaching clients, Sue, is an attractive 38-year-old woman with a master's degree and a mid-level manager's position with her company.

Sue had a huge fairy-tale like church wedding that yielded a marriage that lasted for about eighteen months to a man who had no regard for loving and honoring her. You see, Sue's ex-husband loved himself far more than he could have ever loved Sue.

He was the pretty boy type and was extremely pleased with himself. Not that there is anything fundamentally wrong with a pretty boy; a man cannot help the way he looks, but in this context pretty boy refers to a mentality as much as physical appearance. It was not unusual for Sue's ex-husband not to have money to take her out on dates because dates were not in his budget. However, new outfits, his new shoes, his expensive cologne, his high-end haircuts were expenditures he would not compromise. It was always something for himself. He focused so much on his guise that he would spend more time in the mirror getting dressed than Sue did, and he didn't have hair or make-up to contend with!

Looking back, Sue can admit that she saw all of the

signs before they married but she chose to ignore them. Sue is grateful they never had any children together, thus affording her a clean break from this man without having to stay in contact for the sake of children. Now, we can hope that Sue has learned from this experience and has moved on to date quality men without placing so much emphasis on their appearance. Wrong! Sue's problem is that she continues to seek out that which was problematic in the first place. When questioned about this, Sue only laments that she can't help it; she is attracted to a certain look: a certain height, a certain body build, curly hair, light colored eyes, dressed impeccably, and so on.

Sue needs to break out of the mold. When she begins to look for value and quality, her chances of finding a man who is ideal for her will greatly increase. If you have a track record of dead end relationships, at some point you have to begin to wonder not only what are you attracting, but what is attractive to you. Are you so attracted to a look and an image that you discount everything else? Consider this: the most handsome man you have ever known will not look so good to you after a few years of his mistreating you. Conversely, when you break out of your mold, a man that you were only marginally attracted to at first meeting can develop into the best looking man in your eyes because of how well he treats you. I can't endorse this principal enough and I can tell you from firsthand experience how true this concept is.

When I first met my husband, I was not necessarily physically attracted to him. There was something about his kindness and sense of humor that convinced me to go out with him. As time goes on, my husband becomes more attractive to me because of how well he treats me. So if you are in a mold, break out of it! Stop and think about that something within you that allows you to be continuously attracted to what is obviously not working for you. Expand your dating horizons and see all of the opportunities available to you when you are not focused on the appearance of the vehicle.

CHAPTER 13

Classics Are Still Good for the Trip

For those of us over the age of 30, we should be able to remember what our mothers and grandmothers instilled in us. Do not make yourself so available and do not chase a man. Chasing, more than anything, puts you at a huge disadvantage . Mothers used to teach their daughters not to call a boy; let him call you and show his interest, they'd say. There is something to be said about this approach. When we make ourselves so readily available, the appearance of a desperate woman takes over in a man's mind. Learn how to be kind and show interest without lunging and feeling like you have to chase him down. Even the Bible tells us that when a man finds a wife, he finds a good thing. Let him find you.

While I am a proponent of women's rights from the standpoint of equal pay for equal work, the women's movement may have changed legislation but it did not change how men think. I know too many women who throw themselves at men and then wonder why the men are not interested after a few weeks. I see this happening even with young women. I am the mother of a teenage son and his phone is constantly ringing with girls calling him. When I overhear the conversations, he seems bored and has no real interest in these girls who are calling him because they make themselves too available. They present no challenge. The same applies to women. You have to present yourself as a challenge. When I was in high school there was a phrase "hard to get" which referred to a young lady who did not make it easy to date her.

Guess what; hard-to-get works. In a man's mind, when you don't present a challenge, they can only assume that you make it this easy for any man to date you. Because they are natural born conquerors, they have to believe that they are conquering something that hasn't easily been conquered before, similar to wanting to be the first person to climb a particular mountain or be the first person in space. As women, we don't necessarily relate to this, but trust me on this, men are wired that way. How many women are concerned with getting to the top of a mountain first just so they can stick their stake in the ground and proclaim to the world that they accomplished something that nobody else has been able to do? For a man, being first is a huge feat. Take that same concept and apply it to the world of dating and eventually marriage. When, after the very first meeting, you are constantly calling him, dropping by, or just generally making yourself available without any difficulty at all, he can't feel that sense of challenge that he can work towards conquering.

You have already shown him how easily he can climb your mountain, so the interest is lost; you become a pointless climb. Case in point: Nicole is 41 years old, divorced, with one teenage daughter. She married young to a man who was going into the military. Shortly after their wedding they went oversees together as husband and wife. After about four years, his tour of duty was over, and with that he realized that they really didn't have anything in common, so he divorced Nicole. Unfortunately, after being divorced, Nicole became the poster child for easiness.

Whenever she meets a man, she immediately begins to call him and invite him out on dates or make suggestions that they get together. Usually within the first month of meeting someone, Nicole is sleeping with the guy, and, if the dating goes into the second month, she is already buying Modem Bride magazines and planning the wedding. This is usually when the men she dates lose interest, and she is left feeling broken-hearted and confused over why the relationship didn't work. After all, she tried so hard to show how much she was interested and made herself available to his every want and whim. Nicole has even been left at the altar by a man that she pursued. He allowed Nicole to go into overdrive with the relationship and went along with her desperation, letting her pay for her own engagement ring and plan an entire wedding and reception.

On the day of the wedding, he literally did not show up; this is what nightmares and Hollywood dramas are made of. After an experience like that, you could assume that Nicole has learned from it and does not continue to pursue men like a broke bounty hunter. Wrong! Nicole continues to relentlessly pursue men without regard for letting them come after her. She constantly initiates the phone calls and the dates, and, years after being left at the altar, Nicole continues with the same behavior. Nicole will continue in this pathetic cycle of meeting and hurting until she makes a dramatic change in herself.

When Nicole is finally able to believe that men must do the chasing, then she will be able to potentially attract and hold the interest of a gold man. The advice of old still holds true-let the man come to you. I remember dating as a teenager. When a boy came to my house he had to get out of the car and come speak to my parents before he was allowed to take me out. He couldn't just pull up and blow the horn because that was a sign of disrespect.

As women in the new millennium, we have to get rid of the "blow the horn mentality" and start insisting that men get out of the car to come and date us. The Bible tells us that when a man finds a wife, he finds a good thing. So if the man's job is to find us, doesn't that mean we can relax a bit and let him do the work? The tip is to just make sure you are prepared when he comes to find you. That is why we should focus on loving and developing self so that when he does come looking, we are not caught off guard. Imagine if the man of your dreams were to show up at your door on a Saturday morning when you had decided to sleep in late.

You answer the door in your raggedy pajamas, hair in multiple-colored rollers, sleep in your eyes, teeth not brushed, and your house a mess. At this point, it is too late to do anything about the circumstances. You just have to accept whatever happens because you simply weren't prepared. But if you are able to answer the door in your most flattering outfit with your hair freshly done, your make-up and perfume intact, and your house immaculate, you are ready for come-what-may. Surely, you would rather be ready than not. Consider the old adage that you would rather have "it" and not need "it" than to need "it" and not have "it." Also, remember if you are not sure about how to get ready, it is okay to stop and get directions for your destiny.

CHAPTER 14

Be Careful of the Blind Spots

There are times on the journey when you either cannot or will not see things as they clearly are. When you begin your journey and begin to merge onto the freeway to find true love, it is imperative to utilize not only your peripheral vision but also to make sure you checked your rearview mirror carefully for the blind spots. Failure to yield and to make sure you are aware of everything coming your way will cause you to operate in such a manner that the blind spots of the journey will become the cause of major collisions along the way.

I have had several clients who came to me after a major accident in their relationship. In most cases the situation could have been avoided if they had paid attention to the blind spots on the road. As intelligent, educated women, they could have seen the signs along the way, the indications that major problems were up ahead. Either they did not see it coming, or they allowed the signs to fall into their blind spot of vision. Let me be specific here in that, yes, there are times when we know in our innermost being that something isn't as it should be, but at the time it seems easier to accept than to confront. This is the self-imposed blind spot that could have been seen but was not.

Another term for a blind spot is denial. It seems that in matters of the heart, though, denial is too passé and is so overused in everything from addiction to weight-loss to parenting to responsibility issues. I prefer to identify this issue, not as denial, but as a lack of sight simply because of overt choices to place the concerns out of our line of sight, and willingly create a blind spot to justify our behavior.

Judy is a coaching client who had experienced a number of relationships in which she ended up being the casualty of war. Judy had been married and divorced twice with each marriage resulting in one child. When I met Judy she was the mother of two teenagers and had been divorced for three years. She met a man while buying gasoline and they exchanged phone numbers. Judy had not yet learned how to navigate the early stages of establishing the relationship and immediately began calling the man and suggesting dating opportunities. While a date in the true sense of the word never materialized, Judy would often take a bottle of wine over to his place and the date would consist of her watching television or a movie with him.

This went on for about a month with Judy always being the initiator and the guy just accepting her coming to his house at his convenience. Eventually, they became intimate and began to sleep together after they had finished the bottle of wine. This sexual phase lasted for several months until one fateful evening, after Judy and the guy had sex, he informed her that he was getting married to someone else he had met. Of course, he tried to be mildly decent and admit to Judy that he had only recently met this person, and it just felt right so he decided to take the plunge and marry her. I would bet good money that he had been doing what I like to refer to as "reality dating" his bride-to-be the entire time while Judy became his constant booty call.

I consider it reality dating because the feelings of wanting to date are mutual, and it is a shared reality for both people that there is an interest, not just one person wanting to believe there is a mutual interest, or one person putting on a full court press to create a faux dating scenario. Of course, what the guy did to Judy was wrong, and there are some unkind words we could use to refer to his behavior, but I prefer to stay above the fray of male bashing. Suffice it to say he could have done things differently. Interestingly enough, Judy was heartbroken over this situation. In all truth, instead of being heartbroken, the real emotion should have been self-disappointment. She had allowed herself to become a "place-holder", just helping him bide time and hold a place until his real wife showed up.

Judy's unwillingness to acknowledge the obvious road signs became the reason for her crash. If Judy had been prepared to see what was really going on and had glanced in her rearview mirror just long enough to remember the lessons learned from her past mistakes, her feelings could have been spared. After all, we cannot be upset with God or anyone else if we have sufficient warning and continue along a path that results in disaster. Knowing that something wasn't quite right, Judy was ignoring what I call the Holy Spirit safety net. Anything that happened after she disregarded the warning was her choice, thus her consequence.

Let's take a look at all of the signs along the way that

could have and should have alerted Judy. Notice that when they met, she immediately began calling him. Next, she always suggested dating opportunities, but he declined to take her anywhere or do anything with her other than to allow her to come to his house to participate in what he was already doing anyway, sitting home watching television. Spending time with Judy did not require any investment on his part. He did not have to give of any time or any money; after all, she was even the one supplying the wine. As if all of that was not bad enough, Judy began to have sex with him, which basically sealed her fate to become nothing more than what we have all come to know as a booty call. Judy allowed all of this to happen and yet wanted to blame the entire occurrence on the man. In actuality, he showed Judy exactly who he was and what he wanted; she just refused to see it. I love Maya Angelou's quote, "When people show you who they really are, believe it."

Judy's failure to acknowledge the road signs was one of the reasons for her crash, yet another dimension to consider is how Judy was participating in an emotional realm that permitted her to believe she was heartbroken. I had to ask Judy some tough questions to help her gain understanding about love and broken heartedness. For the sake of someone else who may be experiencing blind spots, I have listed several questions from the Judy scenario to consider:

» What does love defined mean to you?
» When did you come to love this man?
» What was the foundation of this love?
» Tell me what it looks like for a man to show you how much he cares and values you.
» How do you know what love is?
» Describe a basic timeline for the falling in love process.
» How do you reciprocate love?
» Who in your past has demonstrated love to you?
» How do you typically demonstrate love to someone else?

» Tell me about an example of love without sex.
» How about an example of sex without love?

These questions are elements in a process that I used to help Judy to disrobe what was masquerading as a broken heart. Had Judy looked closely, she would have seen the shallow depths of the relationship and its lack of potential for longevity, and in light of such stark reality, she could not have loved what was not there.

As harsh as it may sound, I don't even believe in the concept of "falling in love." You don't fall in love; you fall into a ditch. Instead, love is planted as a seed, and, if nurtured properly, over time it will grow into an amazing and wonderful gift. We must manage our emotions so as to not continue the vicious cycle of hurt because of a misguided belief. In all actuality, falling in love is a false concept perpetuated by every love story we hear on the radio, see on television, or read about in a romance novel. Think about this, if you fall, that means you are walking around temporarily blind and not paying attention to where you are going. The general implication of falling is that an accident has occurred. There isn't any other context in the English language where falling into something is a good thing. Planting a seed, nurturing the seedling until it takes root, and then growing a relationship to allow it to come into full bloom is how I believe true love is established.

Equally as important to blind spots in the journey is utilizing your peripheral vision. Many women I meet are moving full steam ahead without noticing what is going on around them. They are clueless to everyone and everything else. Instead of having blind spots, they aren't even paying attention during the journey. This is just as potentially detrimental because it will also leave you very vulnerable, sitting on the side of the road after a fender bender saying, ouch!

A good friend of my family, Cicely, owns several

rental properties in a neighborhood considered to be very desirable for young couples. Whenever one of the houses becomes available for rent, it is very easy for Cicely and her husband to find qualified tenants, which gives them the luxury of being selective with any of the potential candidates. Recently Cicely told me of an occasion when one of her rental homes became available and she was accepting applications. One woman in particular called her persistently and mentioned several times that the home was perfect for her and her fiancé, so Cicely set an appointment to show them the house. Several days later Cicely showed the house to the woman and her fiancé, both of whom indicated they liked the house. When showing the house, Cicely found it peculiar that for all of the excitement the woman had on the phone about her fiancé, in person with her supposedly soon-to-be hubby, there was a very obvious reserve from her.

When it was time to arrange for the application process, the woman happened to be sitting in the car. Cicely explained to the man that, since they were both renting the house, she would need to run a renters' history for both of them and they would both need to sign the application. Without hesitation the man exclaimed that he did not want her on the lease; it wasn't that kind of relationship and he didn't want the woman thinking that it gave her any entitlement to be at his house. When Cicely relayed this story to me, what struck me was the emphasis she said the man placed on the "her on the lease" and "his house." Isn't that odd, seeing as how the woman considered him her fiancé and had no problem at all referring to them as a couple who wanted to rent the house?

The illustration from my friend Cicely is a classic example of going through life without using any peripheral vision. Certainly if the woman had paid attention to what was going on around her, she would have seen that he did not share the same sentiment toward her as she expressed for him. Now is a great time to identify if your sight needs to be adjusted for the journey. Maybe blind spots have you in a place where you can't or won't see situations as they are, or perhaps you are just not utilizing your peripheral vision. Either way, understand what a critical sense our sight is, and remember it is okay to stop and get directions to your destiny along the way.

CHAPTER 15

Where Is True Love Anyway?

On the journey toward love, some have been traveling longer than others and are beginning to wonder at this point where true love is anyway. Probably the most famous Bible passage concerning love is found in 1 Corinthians 13 where the Apostle Paul describes love in a way that does not mention feelings but an attitude and a mindset. *Think of Love as patience and kindness, not jealousy or boastfulness, not conceitedness, or selfishness, not being easily provoked. And love certainly does not keep score.* None of these attributes require a feeling at the onset either. Instead, these are attitudes that we choose to embrace for ourselves and employ in our relationships with others.

Love actually does not begin with emotions at all, but it starts with the mind and how we determine to think and treat ourselves, as well as those we profess to have feelings for. I am actually grateful that love is not an emotion based on feelings, for if that were the case, we would not have any control over love. We would be at the mercy of others and would only be able to give and receive love based on how other people are able to make us feel.

It is also important to consider that in 1 John 3:18 we are taught not to love with words or tongue, but with actions and in truth. Take this to mean that it is far more important to show love than to talk about love. Please take the time to embrace this concept wholeheartedly while you are on the road to love. Show God how much you love Him by trusting in His word and obeying His commands. Show yourself that you are loved by caring and honoring you. Only when you have shown the love of God and love of yourself should you begin considering how to love your mate. Since actions speak louder than words, and this couldn't be any truer than as it relates to matters of the heart, remember it is always okay if you need to stop and get directions to your destiny.